Wicca Spells

A Beginner's Guide to Wiccan Magic

Table of Contents

Introduction 1

Chapter One: What Is Wicca? 5

Chapter Two: Simple Candle Spells 17

Chapter Three: Spells for True Love 30

Chapter Four: Spells for Luck 37

Chapter Five: Spell for Abundance 43

Chapter Six: Spells for Friendship 50

Chapter Seven: Spells for Peace & The Planet 56

Chapter Eight: Celebrating the Sabbats 66

Conclusion 70

Introduction

When you were a child, you probably spent your days with half a foot in the 'real' world and the other in a world of your own imagination—a place where good things happened simply because you wished them so and where there were no limits on your imagination and Magickal Thinking.

As we grow up and start to plant both feet in the world, many of us lose the joy of running wild with our imaginations and the freedom of living with an open heart.

We begin to conform. We believe what we are told. We lose the ability to think for ourselves and decide for ourselves what's 'real' and what's a construct.

Happily, once you enter the world of Wicca–whatever your age–you regain the magic all children can conjure at will and re-learn the Art of Magickal Thinking.

And that's what this book is all about–it is your guide to finding your way back to the joy and the freedom of making choices and making good things happen, not only for yourself but for those around you; those you love and even those you've never met, but who need your help.

In this *Beginner's Guide to Wiccan Magic,* I'm going to show you how to help and heal yourself and others. Soon, you'll be transferring these skills and using them to help your community, the world, animals, and even the planet itself.

Let's think of this as my guide to you as a 'witch-in-training' with the shared understanding that for us, the word 'witch', does not mean anything bad.

In fact, you can trace it back to its old English roots and the words 'wicca' and *'wicce'*. Wicca was the masculine form, and *wicce* the feminine, but by the Middle Ages both had merged to the word, *'wicche'* which no longer made any distinction between the genders.

You can see it was then just a short step for *wicche* to become the word *witch* that we use today, but what you may not know is the true meaning of the word witch.

The word 'Witch' simply means WISE ONE.

Esoteric (definition) – *intended for, or likely to be understood by only a small number of people with a specialized knowledge or interest*

Witches, male and female, were the once-respected followers of the old Wicca religion, or spiritual path, and as such brought great wisdom, healing, and profound teachings to their communities.

We know that with great knowledge comes great power and so, sadly, there came a time when those with this special knowledge were no longer feted, but were seen as a threat to a mostly Christian and Puritan society.

Those religious societies then set about purging their communities of anyone who did not conform and who could be in possession of any kind of esoteric knowledge. They set brother against sister, neighbor against neighbor, and appealed to the very worst in human nature to ferret out anyone still adhering to Wiccan practices.

You probably know a little about what happened next; witches of both sexes, but primarily women, were accused of practicing the Dark Arts, working against humanity and good Christian values and in league with the very devil himself.

Many witches were brought to trial and brutally executed. And by many, I mean millions. In fact, for the four hundred years that the Christian hysteria over witchcraft loomed large—from the 15th to the 19th century and especially in Europe and New England—an estimated 9 million people, including men, women, and children were accused of being witches and either tortured or burned.

For those Wiccans who remained committed to this ancient path of knowledge and wisdom, this meant taking those teachings and rituals underground, which is where they stayed until the middle of the last century.

The Wiccan teachings were not secret because they were up to no good; they were secret because they were misunderstood and needed protecting.

Happily, today, with modern witchcraft we have access not only to those most ancient teachings but to the reinvigorated post-persecution version of wicca that is so appealing to anyone with a good heart and the desire to make the world a better place for all of us who share it.

In this book, I'll share with you the basic core principles of the wiccan way of life and then teach you some basic spells to help you to release your own Magickal Powers so that you can do your bit to help yourself and others.

I'll make sure you know the basic rules of Magick, so you can't accidentally cause any harm, and I will show you how to cast spells to attract more love, more luck, more abundance, more friendship and more happiness into not only your own life but the lives of those around you.

We have a saying in Wicca which we use to close our circles and to finish casting off our spells.

We say, *"So mote it be."*

Which just means, it is and must be so. In other words, this is the right thing to say and to do.

And, since you've found your way to this book, that's what I am saying to you.

"So mote it be …"

Chapter One: What Is Wicca?

Wiccan (or witchcraft) is an Earth-centered religion, or belief system, based on pre-Christian European traditions. Perhaps one of the oldest of all the religions, its origins can be traced right back to Paleolithic roots (roughly 2.5 million years ago) and to peoples who, back then, worshipped a Fertility Goddess and a Hunter God.

Today, Wicca takes all its teachings from nature. So much of the witchcraft practiced by modern Wiccans is all about working with and alongside the positive and life-affirming forces of nature that sustain life in all its forms.

That doesn't mean you have to live in the countryside and the middle of nowhere to practice wicca—you don't; but as you work your way through the spells in this book you will feel a deepening of your own connections with the natural world on your doorstep—the world you see going quietly about its business from your window or at the bottom of your backyard. This deeper connection, with the life forces that sustain all life, is just one of the joys of a wiccan practice.

Sometimes called Modern Witchcraft—despite having pagan roots stretching back eons—Wicca resurfaced in England in the 1940s and 1950s where a devotee and retired British civil servant, Gerald Gardner re-introduced the wiccan path to the public, calling it "The Craft of the Wise."

Wiccan beliefs

Modern Wicca is also classified as one of the Mystery Religions because it encompasses the practice of magic (sometimes spelled *magick*) and rituals and spells. While outsiders, and those unfamiliar with the core beliefs of modern wiccans, may fear notions of witchcraft and sorcery; the modern witch will tell you they work only for the greater good.

There is one simple but powerful reason you can believe they are telling the truth and that is because one of the fundamental rules that governs any modern practice of witchcraft is the 'Rule of Three' which states that whatever energy a person deliberately puts out into the world—positive or negative—will be returned back to them; not once; not twice, but threefold!

Other religions refer to this idea as the Law of Karma. However, not all these religions also practice the 'Rule of Three'. So, maybe think twice before doing anything wicked.

As we work our way through this beginner's guide to casting spells, we will always be working with the Rule of Three, which just means the more 'good' we put out into the world, the more 'good' will come back to us.

Wiccan 'worship'

Wiccans don't spend too much time thinking about the Afterlife. They're more interested in being the best version of themselves in this life. While they do worship 'deities' they see them as being part of this world and not the next.

The two main 'characters' today's practitioners pay their respects to are the Triple Goddess and the Horned God.

You can think of The Triple Goddess as representing the 'feminine' and in particular, the three distinct stages of a woman's life; childhood and young adulthood (Maid); maturity (Mother) and older age (Crone).

The passage from one life stage to the next is perfectly natural and wiccans honor old age and the hard-won wisdom that comes with it as much as they honor youth with all its energy. In ritual and spells, we refer to The Triple Goddess as simply The Goddess.

The Horned God is a representation of the 'masculine.' He is seen as the consort and companion of The Goddess, and is strongly associated with nature and the wilderness, sexuality/fertility, and hunting.

While we may be using the terms 'Goddess' and 'God,' it's important to understand that we're not talking about actual deities—for wiccans, these are more archetypes that represent characteristics and qualities we can choose to honor and respect and call on to help us with our wiccan work.

The big word here is 'choose', because wicca, more than many other traditions, encourages choice. When we embark on this path, the second most important rule—after making sure you cause no harm—is to do nothing that doesn't feel authentic and right for you.

Wiccan symbols

A symbol is just a mark; a sign; a word; or an object that we use to represent an idea. It's an object or a relationship and, in the spells we will learn through this book, we will use symbols to represent our growing relationship to the energy of both The Goddess and The Horned God.

We can be as creative as we like when it comes to choosing and making these symbols—which is a huge part of the joy of Wicca. But, we can also look to wiccan traditions for ideas about the symbols we want to use when casting spells and doing our good works.

We've seen already how The Goddess is linked with the powerful female energies of creation and, so often, the symbol we use for her is the moon.

You may come across a powerful wiccan symbol called the triple moon; this depicts a full moon in the center and a sickle moon on each side. The triple moon represents the Triple Goddess and the three stages of womanhood described above.

You can easily draw this symbol to connect you to the Goddess energy when you do your wiccan work but there are numerous other traditional symbols for the Goddess including: an apple, a cowrie shell, a serpent, a rose, a circle, and even just the color black.

Sometimes, The Horned God has been misrepresented as being a symbol of the devil but of course, he's not—rather, he's a symbol of the magical powers of life; of rebirth, reunion, hope, and even salvation.

The symbol of the Horned God is the Sun. He is sometimes depicted as The Stag. And because he is so powerfully linked with nature, you can actually use anything you bring into your home from the natural world to connect to that energy including a small branch from a holly or oak tree (he has also been known as The Holly King and the Oak King). Or you can simply draw a set of stag antlers and make that the symbol of the masculine energies you will be working with.

The Pentacle

How many horror films invoke the Dark Arts by depicting a pentacle scrawled on the bathroom mirror or the floor of a nasty murder scene? The answer is too many.

For Wiccans, the pentacle is a symbol of faith that is as meaningful as the symbol of the cross is to those practicing the Christian faith. At its simplest, the pentacle is a five-pointed star set within a circle with each of the five points representing the five elements of spirit, air, earth, fire, and water and the circle itself representing the universe.

You can make a pentacle from anything you like, and if you want to see one made in nature, next time you pick up an apple, cut it in half precisely down the center of its core; separate the two halves and take a look at the arrangement of the seeds inside!

Wiccan 'tools'

Your symbols are just one of the important tools you'll be using when you start to cast your spells. Let's explore some of the other things you might find useful to work with. Remember though, there are no hard and fast rules here. You do not need to go out and spend $$$ on fancy witchy accessories—you can start small and build up your 'toolbox'. As we go through each item you might like to consider acquiring, I'll suggest some homemade alternatives that you might want to start your Wiccan journey with. This is wise because you'll discover you have more of a feeling for one type of work over another. Like I said, no hard and fast rules here—except of course, the basic rules about responsibility and making sure you do no harm.

The one important thing to keep in mind is that your witchy tools all serve the same primary function, which is to assist you in focusing your intention.

Focusing intention = the essence of true Magick

Sacred Altar Space

Your altar is the sacred space you create to cast your spells and work your Magickal miracles. The key word here is 'space.' You can make an altar from an old bedside cupboard in the corner of the bedroom or turn a tubby box, which holds your Magickal tools, upside down; cover it with a special cloth that you don't use for anything else—and hey, presto! You have a portable altar.

As in life, don't sweat the small stuff. Your altar can be whatever you want and wherever you want but it is important. You choose one space for your indoor work and always use that space if you can, to cast your indoor spells. The reason this matters is because energy—which cannot be either created or destroyed—can be built up. Think of this as being like you add a new layer of your own Magickal energy and personality to the proceedings every time you cast a spell, using the same tools in the same space. It won't be long before you will come to feel, in every part of your body, that this has become a special and sacred space for you.

You can keep all your Magickal tools, talismans and symbols on your altar, and in this space, so that as soon as you step into it, you feel the energy shift.

I would suggest too that you keep it private and special. Don't show it off because you don't want someone else's energy (or intent) intruding. This space and this altar are just for you.

Candle(s)

In the next chapter I will introduce you to the joy of casting simple candle spells; but if you think about it, you've probably done this before without even thinking about it.

Did anyone ever make you a special birthday cake and then invite you to blow out the birthday candles? What do they tell you to do as you blow? They tell you to make a wish.

This is a Magickal ritual that many of us have been lucky enough to participate in—either as children or as adults then teaching it to children—without even realizing we were summoning and releasing our Magickal powers at all.

You can buy beautiful and ready-made Magickal Spell candles (maybe treat yourself to one or two next birthday). You can also just as easily make your own.

Candle Magic is a really good way of starting out on your Wiccan path. Whatever candle you use, it will do two things as you light it:

> (1) Your candle will help you focus your intent and keep that focus as you cast your spell.
>
> (2) The flame will both honor and invoke the divine energies you like to work with—The Triple Goddess or the Horned God—or even the animal and ancestor spirits you feel can help you with your Wiccan work.

Even the color of the candle you choose to work with is symbolic, and in the next chapter—where I'll teach you how to cast candle spells—we'll learn how to use the different colors to match with our specific intent.

Wand

You probably had one of these as a child too, again, without really realizing that's what it was or why it was important to you. Did you have a favorite stick? Did you cling to it long after your parents told you to ditch it? Did you use your beloved stick to poke at the flames of a campfire or to toast marshmallows?

Any stick that comes to some kind of point at the end can be used as a wand, which is simply a physical device designed to send energy from your body, down through your arm, hand, and then through the stick (wand) and out into the universe as part of your Magickal intent/spell.

Without your energy and intent, a stick is just—well—a stick. The same can be said for the fanciest of wands. With your energy and intent, we have something sacred and special.

Your wand is a symbol of Air.

Cauldron/Burner

Some people will use the word cauldron, and others will freak out at the word. Yet, historically, a cauldron was an everyday item—a large, cast iron cooking pot that a witch could use to simmer a stew by day and then mix up a Magickal potion by night. So, you can see, there is nothing to fear with this word. Anyway, it is up to you what you call the vessel you choose that allows you to change energy by burning or boiling. You could even use an old saucepan and, if you don't have any other heat source, place it on the kitchen hob to do your Magickal works. In Wicca, the cauldron represents the womb of The Goddess—a fertile place where ideas and creations can simmer and stew.

In more advanced Magickal spells, you can use your cauldron to represent the elements of fire and water in your work.

Athame (Dagger)

Athame is a word used to describe a knife or blade, one that most usually has a black handle and one that you only use in your Magickal rituals. You're not going to need one of these for your beginner spells, but one may find its way to you as you progress down the Wiccan path. In that, this is often what happens—somehow, the right 'tool' just appears when the time is right. This makes it more special than simply finding something in an online shop. Don't worry about an athame for now but just be confident you know what one is.

In the Tarot traditions, the dagger or athame or sword represents Air and the intellect—your wits, if you like. This is not a weapon and must never, ever be used to draw blood. If you have an accident with it and blood is spilled, the symbol has been tainted and must be replaced.

Chalice

Just a fancy word for cup or drinking vessel. You won't be drinking anything from your chalice, but it is an important symbol of water and of the Goddess so it should sit on your altar to keep your focus/intent on her Magickal powers which you will invoke as you cast your spells. In more advanced spells, the chalice may be used to hold wine and is seen as symbolic of the womb of the Goddess. For you, just starting out, it is just a symbol of her presence throughout nature and her willingness to help you to do good in the world.

Broomstick

Witches may have been accused of flying about on broomsticks (a suggestion that has more to do with using psychoactive herbs that facilitate astral projections and travel in advanced witchcraft) but it is true that the humble household broom was and remains important to those practicing the Craft of the Wise.

One reason is that witches treat their environment as an extension of their physical bodies, so a clean home presents a purity of intent and an unsullied heart. Happily, you can use your everyday broom symbolically in your Wicca work.

When casting a circle for spells, witches would swing their broomsticks back and forth as they walked the circle. The idea was that this would cast out negative energy in preparation for spellcasting. The broom itself was also a symbol of the coming together of male and female energies in spell-work, with the bristles representing feminine energies and the handle representing masculine. Even if you do no more than sweep the floor where you practice your craft, you are using a Magickal tool when you use your household broom!

Consecrating your tools

Consecrating both your Magickal tools and the sacred space you plan to use to cast your spells is important for two reasons; firstly, it removes any negative energies and secondly, it purifies everything you'll be bringing before the Divine energies you'll be working with. Consecrating your space and your tools also brings Divine blessings to your work.

Herbal Apothecary

With these beginner spells, you will be also using herbs in your spell-work. You might only ever think about herbs when you cook and want to add flavor to your dishes, but all plants have Magickal and mystical properties which we can easily harness in our Wiccan works.

Here is a list of the herbs you will need for the spells that follow in this book:

- Lavender
- Dried Bay Leaves
- Rosemary
- Cinnamon sticks
- Sage
- Parsley
- Thyme

You will be using essential oils in your spell-work too.

Make sure you have:

- Frankincense
- Myrrh
- Lavender
- Lemon Balm
- Rose
- Sage

Your Most Important 'Tool'

When you start out as a new Wiccan Witch, you have a unique 'tool' that is more important than anything you can buy or stumble across in nature to help you to focus your intent and to strengthen the magick of your spells and that 'tool' is: **You.**

Try and bring the best version of you into your spell casting circle at all times.

Step into your sacred space with love and authenticity.

Keep your heart open and willing to learn and as you invite the hidden divine forces into your world to help you with this work. Remember to thank them for that help and stay grateful that you're one of the blessed ones who has found the way to take their first steps on their sacred path.

Chapter Two: Simple Candle Spells

Casting a circle

In the Wicca tradition, we cast a circle for all of our Magickal work. I will share with you how to do that. Before you go on to the equally important task of consecrating your altar, the sacred space where you will work indoors, and your sacred tools.

You will need to cast your circle before you move on to that ritual.

But, before we get started, let's just think about why a circle is important to our work and why we cast one?

Firstly, the circle is symbolic—it has no beginning, no middle and no end.

It is a place where all are equal and a protective space that allows us to build the energy of our intent inside its protective circumference.

When you cast your circle, you can literally draw it on the ground and stand in it or you can just indicate the shape with your pointed finger and then imagine yourself standing in it. (Once you have consecrated your tools, you can use your wand or your athame instead of your finger but for now, a digit will do!)

Before you 'draw' your circle, you are going to invite your helpers who will assist; this can be The Goddess, The Horned God, your ancestors, your familiar (an animal soul or spirit you are particularly attached to) plant spirits, nature devas or anything/one else you want to work with.

Invite them graciously, as you would a good friend. And once you have stepped into your circle, do not step out of it again until the Magick is done, and your helpers have departed.

Calling in the Elements and the Cardinal Directions

Before we cast a circle, we call in not only our Divine Helpers but other forces of nature—especially those unseen—that can help us with our magical work. To do that we start by calling in the four directions: East, South, West, and North.

'Calling in' just means issuing an invitation. You can do this verbally, or you can clap your hands towards each direction or beat a shamanic drum. Do what feels right to you.

Calling in the East

The East represents the element of Air and so is linked to ideas, the intellect, and the higher mind.

Light a white candle and turn to face the East. Use your athame (dagger) or a feather to move the air in front of you and invite the East to your circle with the following words:

"East, if it is right for you so, to do; and if you would like to help me then please come into my Magickal circle today."

Calling in the South

The South represents the element of Fire and so is linked to passion and creativity.

Light a red candle. Turn to face the South. Use your wand (once you have consecrated it) to cut through the energy ahead of you and invite the South to your circle with the following words:

"South, if it is right for you so, to do; and you would like to help me then please come into my Magickal circle today."

Calling in the West

The West represents the element of Water and so is linked to emotions.

Light a blue candle. Turn to face the West. If you have consecrated your tools, then use your chalice, or some other small vessel filled with water. Take a sip, swallow and then invite the West with the following words:

"West, if it is right for you so, to do; and you would like to help me then please come into my Magickal circle today."

Calling in the North

The North represents the earth and so symbolizes practical and material matters.

Light a green candle. Turn to face the North. Once you have consecrated your tools, and if you have one, pick up your pentacle symbol. If you don't have one, don't worry. You can use (and consecrate) a small stone or a small tub of earth in the same way. Keep your gaze on your symbol and invite the North with the following words:

"North, if it is right for you so, to do; and you would like to help me then please come into my Magickal circle today."

You have now summoned all four directions and you're ready to cast your circle. But notice, before you do that, that you do not simply impose your will, in any way, to get the help you would like. You have invited your divine helpers; you have invited the elements and the cardinal directions. You have even said 'If it is right so to do' by which you mean 'if you support my intent and the magick I am about to make.'

Absolutely everything you now do, as you cast and step into your circle, must be for the greater good—of yourself and of others.

Creating your circle

You've issued all your invites and now you're ready to welcome all the important guests who will support you as you find your Magickal feet.

Start by facing the East and welcome the element of Air and the East itself. Turn a quarter circle in a clockwise direction and welcome the South and the element of fire. Turn another quarter of a circle, again keeping to a clockwise rotation, and welcome the West and the element of water. Finally, complete your Magickal Circle by turning the last quarter, clockwise, to welcome the North and the element of Earth. Welcome and thank all these elements for coming, and welcome and thank your Divine Helpers too.

You have cast your Magickal circle and can now step into it.

Consecrating your tools and space

It is important to consecrate your tools—and the indoor space where you will be working—to make sure all the energy that is present when you are casting a spell is pure. You wouldn't expect someone to come visit and sleep on dirty sheets in the guest bed and in the same way, you don't want to invite your divine helpers to share either dirty tools or a dirty space with you, so it really is worth taking the time for this ritual.

Plus, it will make you feel like a proper 'witch-in-training' so you will enjoy each step of this important ritual.

For the consecration ritual You will need:

- Incense
- A candle
- A small bowl of water
- Salt

Incense: This represents the East and Air

Candle: This represents the South and Fire

Small bowl of water: This represents the West and Water

Small bowl of salt: This represents the North and Earth

After casting your circle, light the incense and the candle and pick up the tool you wish to consecrate and make sacred. Turn to face the east, pass your tool through the incense smoke and say:

"Powers of the East

Guardians of the Air

I consecrate this [say the name of your tool]

And charge it with your energies.

I purify it and make it sacred."

Now turn to face the South and pass your tool through the candle flame. (Do not do this if you are consecrating something flammable; visualize it being cleansed in the flame instead). Say out loud:

"Powers of the South

Guardians of the Flame

I consecrate this [say the name of your tool]

And charge it with your energies.

I purify it and make it sacred."

Turn to the West and pass your ritual tool over the water in the vessel. Say out loud:

"Powers of the West

Guardians of the Water

I consecrate this [say the name of your tool]

And charge it with your energies.

I purify it and make it sacred."

Turn to face the North. Pass your tool over the salt and say:

"Powers of the North

Guardians of the Air

I consecrate this [say the name of your tool]

And charge it with your energies.

I purify it and make it sacred."

Claiming sacred ownership:

Now face your altar and say:

"I charge this [insert the name of your tool] in the name of the Old Ones

The Ancients, the Sun, the Moon and the Stars

By the powers of Air, Fire, Water and Earth

I banish the energies of any previous owners and make it fresh and new.

I consecrate this [insert name of the tool] and make it sacred and mine."

Keep your consecrated Magical tools in a safe place and away from the energies of others. Each time a new tool finds its way to you—and they will—take the time to consecrate it before you use it for Magickal work.

As you gain confidence in your Wiccan works, you will probably find yourself modifying both these rituals in ways that are unique to you and how you like to work.

Whatever way you work, remember to say your 'pleases' and 'thank yous.'

Closing the Circle

You've probably guessed that we don't go to all this trouble to cast a circle simply to step out of it if the phone rings or we remember our favorite TV show is about to start. Magickal work is serious work and deserves our respect.

When your work is finished, you need to close the circle before you step out of it by thanking all the elements and elementals that have shown up to help enhance your magick and take it out into the universe.

If you're not sure how to say your 'Magickal thank yous' and bid your special guests goodbye, you can copy this closing ritual. Before long, you'll have your own way of both casting and closing your circles.

To close your Magickal Circle, this time, we start where we finished up before, by facing North. Say out loud:

"I thank you Guardians and Powers of the North for attending this circle

You are always welcome here

Go in peace."

Take a quarter turn in an anticlockwise direction to face West and repeat the same thanks.

"I thank you Guardians and Powers of the West for attending this circle

You are always welcome here

Go in peace."

Take a quarter turn in an anticlockwise direction to face South and repeat the same thanks.

"I thank you Guardians and Powers of the South for attending this circle

You are always welcome here

Go in peace."

Blow out your candle.

Repeat your thanks in the same way to the direction and the elements of the East.

Your circle is now closed.

Candle Magick

In the same way you can consecrate our other sacred tools, you can also consecrate the candles we are using in our spell-work. Before you do that, you can choose to work with a candle whose very color represents the essence of your spell. If you are casting a love spell, for example, you would work with a candle that is pink and which, once consecrated, will work to open the energy of the heart chakra (a chakra is an invisible energy center in the body) and to attract romance towards you.

If your spell is about protection, you would use a black candle to help clear negativity and protect you and your living space.

Here is a list of candle colors and what they signify once you start your Magickal work. Remember too, you can change what the candle represents for you. You can infuse it with an essential oil or carve Magickal symbols into the wax. Experiment as you start to cast your spells and see what works best for you.

Candle colors chart

Black—protection

Green—fertility and financial success

Pink—romantic love

White—purity and truth

Red—passion and creativity

Light blue—peace and healing

Brown—earthy and grounding

Dark blue—emotional healing and intuition

Orange,—success and finding your life purpose

Purple—magic and spiritual growth

Silver—psychic insights and abilities

Candle Spells

Candle spells are perfect for beginners because they connect you to Magick; both your own and the unseen Magickal forces that surround us without overwhelming you.

That said, there are a few more basic rules before you try any kind of Magickal spell.

1) Don't start something you can't finish.

2) Don't talk about your Wiccan work, except to others on the path. Witches who work alone are known as Hedgerow Witches and as you start out, that's what you are.

3) Be precise. If you ask for money, make sure you ask that it comes to you without causing harm to anyone else. You don't want a loved one to die and leave you their money as an inheritance. Yes, your wish has come true and the Magick has worked—but at what cost?

4) Remember, too, the Rule of Three. That anything that harms one, harms all!

You're ready for your first Candle Spell!

You now have everything you need to cast your first spell which is going to be a candle spell.

First, choose the color of the candle that is the best fit with your wish/intent. If, for example, you've found yourself wobbling and feeling agitated by the relentless doom and gloom of a news agenda dominated by a worldwide pandemic; you may, perhaps, choose a brown candle to help you regain your equilibrium and make you feel your feet are back on *terra firma.*

Experienced Wiccans work with and understand the cycles of the moon. But for starters, just keep in mind that if you want to draw something to you, start your spell work on the New Moon and if you want to banish or dispel something, do it after the Full Moon when the moon is waning.

You are going to write your desire/wish/intent on your candle once you have consecrated it and so, again, there are some simple guidelines to follow.

If you want to draw something towards you, write down what that is, starting at the top of the candle and writing all the way down along the length of it. Again, to dispel something, write in the opposite direction, from the bottom of the candle up to the top.

Candle Magic works well in the dark so cast your circle and light your consecrated candle. Imagine, in your mind's eye, what it is you want to happen. Spend as long doing this as feels right and when you have finished, blow your candle out and be ready to do the same again the next night.

You will repeat this simple spell every night until the moon has finished waxing or waning, depending on whether you're drawing something to you or dispelling it. At the end of this spell, bury or burn what is left of the candle. Don't just bin it.

Do not tell anyone about your spell. Just wait patiently and let your helpers and the universe work their Magick.

"So, mote it be"

Chapter Three: Spells for True Love

We've consecrated our sacred tools, prepared the space and our altar and know how to cast a circle for spellwork, which can only mean one thing—we're good to go! Over the next chapters, I will share some simple beginner's Wiccan spells to attract more of what you want into your life, plus some spells that are all about helping others—your local community and even the planet itself.

So, let's start with the one topic everyone asks about—spells for true love.

For this spell you will need pink candles, a small spell jar with a cork or screw-top lid to make an air-tight seal, dried bay leaves, a red pen, a rose quartz crystal or, if you don't have one, a rose flower or the image of a rose; you will also need white sage incense for cleansing your workspace, plus the herbal ingredients listed below for each of the spells. Before you start any spell work, make sure you have carefully read the list of things you'll need for your spell casting to go smoothly, and prepare them in advance—in the same way you would do '*mis en place*' and chop everything in advance if you were preparing an elaborate meal. You don't want to have to leave/break the circle because you've forgotten an important herbal ingredient or don't have somewhere to safely place your burning spell candle whilst you cast the spell with your wand.

Notice too how these are spells for true love, not just any old love. This means you must feel ready and able to make the space in your life for a committed relationship before you cast any of these spells. If you're not ready yet, that's fine, move on to one of the other chapters and come back to this one when your heart tells you to.

Remember too, the most important tool you'll ever use when casting spells is your own belief that they will work and what you ask for will be granted to you. If you don't believe, Wicca is not for you. I'll also reiterate that what happens after you've cast your spell is not up to you. Your desire will go out into the 'Web of Fate' that connects us all; what you get back will be what you need right now.

The best day to cast Love spells is on a Friday

Love Spell #1

If you want to attract love, any good witch will tell you that this spell should therefore be cast between the New Moon and the Full Moon—and not once the moon is waning. It is important we get into the habit of working in harmony with nature—not against her—and as you progress, you'll become more skilled at this and at knowing when it's the right time, or tide, or season to cast your spells out into the world.

You are not working with your own will, but the will of the Divine energies you invite into your circle to help strengthen your Magickal work.

Candle: Pink or red

You can make your own Love Candle and even carve the name of the person you want to attract to you if you have someone particular in mind. Remember, you cannot impose your will on someone else (or the universe) so this is an invitation to 'join you in true love' and not a spell to make anyone do anything they don't want to do.

If you don't have someone specific in mind, you can just carve a heart on your candle and the words *'True Love to Me'* down the length, running from the top to the bottom because you want to draw this toward you.

To cast:

Invite your Divine helpers to work with you to draw love to you

Cast your circle and stand tall in the center of it.

Put your right hand over your heart and close your eyes.

Try to imagine your heart expanding and opening up ready to receive true love

Open your eyes, remove your hand from your heart and feel your breath settle into a calming rhythm.

Enjoy this peaceful sense of union with your own heart

Feel the loving feelings that you will offer to a new partner

Now, light your Love Spell candle and say out loud:

> *"If it pleases, I am now open to true love and ready to *romantically share my life with a new lover; please send this love to me."*

Allow yourself to imagine this new love taking your hand and you theirs and see, in your mind's eye, the pair of you leaping ahead into Life's Great Adventure together.

Sit or stand quietly in your circle and watch as your 'Love Candle' burns down.

When it feels right, finish your spell with the words that witches all over the land will say before they end a spell and close a circle; say out loud:

"So, mote it be"

Now close your circle and thank all those invisible helpers you have worked with you today.

Take the candle stub and store it somewhere safe.

Now forget about your spell and trust that what/who is right for you will come your way when the time is right for them too.

**The word 'romantically' is important here because otherwise, you might get sent more loving friends or relatives when what you want is someone to be in love with who will love you right back and want to build a relationship with you.*

Love Spell #2

The Magickal properties of the bay leaf are used to manifest our dreams and desires. You can cast a circle and do this spell indoors; or you can find somewhere private outside and carry out this ritual under the great Father Sky.

What you will need:

- dried (large) bay leaf
- small pink or red candle (you can use a small birthday candle or a dedicated spell one)
- rose quartz crystal, a real rose flower or an image of a rose
- red pen
- rose oil
- a bowl of dried lavender

How to cast your spell:

1. Before you start your spell, cleanse your space if you are working indoors. You can use incense to do this; or drumming; or chanting; or you can play music that is sacred to you.

2. Now, cast your circle the way you learned in chapter two.

3. If you plan to cast this spell outside, prepare the candle and the bay leaf and go outside to a private place once both are ready for the spell.

3. Take your pink candle and smother it in rose oil (this will smell divine!).

4. Now roll your scented candle in the dried lavender to 'dress' it.

3. Light the candle and pick up the rose quartz crystal which you are going to hold in your right hand while you set your intentions.

Say, out loud:

"If it pleases, I am now open to true love and ready to romantically share my life with a new lover; please send this love to me."

Now say:

"So, mote it be"

4. Write this same intention on the bay leaf—keep it short and simple—using the red pen.

5. Burn the bay leaf in the flame of the candle, continuing to repeat your intentions.

6. Leave the candle to burn until it's finished.

7. Thank your Divine Helpers, whether you've been working outside or indoors, and if the latter, close the circle.

Chapter Four: Spells for Luck

Luck. What a funny little four-letter word and one with such big connotations. The dictionary definition of luck is that it relates to success of failure which happens outside of your control. In other words, you are lucky or not.

People talk about 'Lady Luck' as if she's a person sitting somewhere out of sight deciding your fate. And you'll have heard people use phrases like 'unlucky in love' and 'you make your own luck' so the spells I will share with you here are really just to nudge luck—good luck—your way and remind 'Lady Luck', wherever she is, that you sometimes need a helping hand.

These spells, the way we cast them, and the herbs we use in these rituals, are only about improving your luck or, if you prefer, your good fortunes. Once you have mastered casting them for yourself, you may want to cast to help someone you know who would benefit from a big dose of better luck. Maybe you know someone who's just lost their job or a family member or who just feels like life never goes their way. You can cast for them by keeping their name in mind during the ritual and maybe placing something of theirs—a photo or a gift they gave you—on your altar so their energy becomes part of your spellcasting. Only do this if the spell is to send more luck toward them. Otherwise, decorate your altar before you start with things that make you feel lucky; this can be coins or crystals, or something precious that unexpectedly came your way like a birthday gift from someone that arrived out of the blue.

The important thing is just to reconnect with that feeling of luck so you can summon it into the circle as you work.

The best day to cast spells for Luck is on a Sunday

Good Luck Spell #1

You're going to choose a candle to cast a candle spell but that means, before you start, you need to be more specific in your own thinking about what would make you feel more lucky or more fortunate.

Are you seeking financial prosperity? More happiness? Better security in your job?

You need to think about this because your answer will determine the color of the candle you will use in this simple spell. While you're trying to work out the answer to this question, why not get your crayons out and draw a symbol of luck—like a four-leaved clover—to place on your altar to represent the luck you want to come into your life (or someone else's.)

If you're struggling to come up with a definitive answer about the type of luck or good fortune you want to specifically attract, just choose between one of these two symbolic candle colors:

Lucky Candle Colors

Green—fertility and financial success

Orange—success and finding your life purpose

Again, as with the True Love spell in the previous chapter, you can either make your own Good Luck candle or use the color that symbolizes your intent—to attract more good luck into your life—and make it bespoke with carvings, either symbols (like the four-leafed clover) or words.

And again, you want to attract this good luck towards you so if you write on the candle; start at the top and write the words down the length of the candle to the bottom.

To cast:

Invite your Divine helpers to work with you to draw Good Luck to you.

Cast your circle and stand tall in the center of it.

Light your Good Luck candle and as it starts to burn, thank your divine helpers for showing up to work with you to cast this spell.

Bring your focus to the symbol for good fortune that you have already placed on your altar and if you use a wand, pick that up now and point it towards that symbol.

Try to imagine a big brick wall that has stood in the way of you receiving the good luck that is available to you (as it is to everyone), and in your mind's eye, just demolish that wall. Blow it up, bulldoze it, do whatever you need to do to knock that wall down.

Now, state your intent and say out loud:

> *If it pleases, I am now open to Good Fortune and ready to receive my share of *Good Luck, please send it to me."*

As you state your clear intent, keep your wand pointing to the symbol of good fortune on your altar and imagine the heavens opening and that same symbol raining down and filling the space ahead of you.

Enjoy this moment of imagining all this good luck coming your way; so much good luck you won't even need to use it up all at once; you can store some for other times and even give some of it away.

If you're not already smiling, you will be soon because just knowing that good luck is on its way to you will make your heart happy.

Now, say the words that witches all over the land will say before they end a spell and close a circle. Say out loud:

"So, mote it be"

Take the Good Luck candle stub and store it somewhere safe.

Now forget about your spell and trust that whatever good luck that is right for you will come your way when the time is right.

*Notice that I have never used the word Luck without the word 'Good' in front of it. We use the same idea of Luck for good luck and bad luck, and we don't want to invite any of the latter into the circle or our lives.

Good Luck Spell #2

For this spell, we are going to make a Dream Pillow that you will keep under your normal pillow from the time of the New Moon to the arrival of the Full Moon, after which you will take it and bury it outdoors, somewhere safe and private where it won't be disturbed.

You can get as creative as you like with this spell, in fact the more creative, the better. The most important thing is that as you work to make your Dream Pillow, you keep in mind the clear intent that you wish more good fortune to come into your life.

The best way to make this feel even more like the sacred activity that it is, would be for you to cast a circle and sit in the middle of it to make your Dream Pillow. As ever, prepare your Magickal '*mis en place*' so you can be sure you have everything you need and won't need to break or leave the circle once cast.

You will need a small piece of plain white cotton; (you can cut this from an old bed sheet but make sure you've washed it) cut into a small rectangle of about 20cm x 10cm. The exact measurements don't matter but you will find it easier to work with a rectangle shape than a square. You will also need a needle and thread because once you have your 'pillow' shape you need to stitch it, fill it, and then stitch the Magickal contents safely inside.

Use fabric pens to decorate the fabric itself with meaningful symbols—you could draw the four-leaved clover again—and when you fold the pillow into shape, make sure your symbols are on the inside and hidden.

Now you can fill your Dream Pillow with the Magickal herbs that will help attract more good fortune your way.

These can include:

Mint— for luck and money

Jasmine—which helps with dreamwork

Sage —for the wisdom to recognize and be grateful for your Good Fortune when she shows up

Holly is also used as a symbol of good fortune, but you don't want a prickly Holly leaf lurking under your pillow so maybe just draw Holly leaves on the cotton pouch you are making and again, hide these symbols inside.

Also, when it comes to Magickal herbs, you can use fresh or dried flowers and leaves interchangeably and if you can't find the plant itself, you can use it as an essential oil—which might be the case here with the Jasmine. If you do that, just add three small drops to the mint and sage mix that is going into your Dream Pillow.

Your Dream Pillow is really a Magickal tool. So, once you have finished making it, you can consecrate it in the exact same way you consecrate all your sacred tools.

As the New Moon rises, put your Dream Pillow under your normal pillow and let it work its Magick. Just make sure you remove it by the Full Moon because we don't want good luck to wane and head the other way—away from you.

You won't use this pillow again so bury it out of sight or burn it and release the ashes, with thanks, to Mother Earth.

Chapter Five: Spell for Abundance

It is important to remember when casting spells to be very specific about your intent and/or what it is you are asking for. So, if you are going to ask for abundance then think about the specific areas of your life where 'more' would be a good thing. Do you need more money? Would you like more work? Are you asking for more happiness?

What would you like an abundance of?

I'll tell you a little story about a newbie Wicca, someone just like you, who couldn't wait to cast a spell for abundance. They were just starting out selling homemade crafts and wanted to ask their Divine Helpers for a Magickal 'boost' to get her new business launched.

They cast the spell I am going to share with you here and within a few weeks, got the boost they had asked for when a local shop placed a huge order with them. The only problem was the wholesale price the shop was willing to pay was dire, which meant the newbie Wicca would be working well below the minimum wage.

The trainee Wicca found herself accepting the paltry offer and working for a pittance for weeks to fulfil that big order. But she never ever forgot the lesson about being more specific—and next time she cast the exact same abundance spell, she remembered to make it clear she wanted more work but she wanted the offers to be fairly priced so she could earn a living and sustain herself!

Here is the dictionary definition of 'Abundance'—a very large quantity of something!

If what you are seeking is Spiritual Abundance—by which we mean a greater appreciation of life in all its fullness and greater strength in your body, mind, and soul—then be very clear about that. Material Abundance and Spiritual Abundance are not the same thing.

Any spells where you are asking specifically for <u>more</u> of something are best done on Thursdays

Abundance Spell Jar

You are going to love, love, love making spell jars. These are a simple, but powerful, tool that you keep by your side until the spell has come to pass. You can make one for yourself or for someone you care about and keep it safely for them. You can use a spell jar to ask for anything—as long as your intent is pure, and you understand what you're asking for will only be granted if it is right for you and it's the right time.

Remember, whatever the spell we cast and whichever method we choose to do so, Wicca is about working with our Divine Helpers and nature, and never about imposing our ego or will on anyone or anything.

Once you have your Spell Jar, keep it close by—in a bedside drawer or in the bag you use most days; keep it secret and don't open the jar, no matter how tempted you are.

You can, of course, also cast for abundance in any of the ways you've learned in the preceding chapters, but making a Spell Jar in and of itself is a Magickal task and one that requires a full Wicca ritual if you want the spell to work.

You can buy small spell jars online and will probably pay less for them if you don't shop at the Wicca store but just check out amazon instead.

Choose very small jars and make sure they come with lids/corks or some other permanent seal.

To make a spell jar

Prepare/tidy/clean the Magickal space you will be working in and when you are ready, invite your Divine Helpers to join you.

You may, now you have already cast several spells, feel a particular attachment to one helper and if so, ask them specifically to come and work with you to create more abundance in your life.

Make sure you are ready to cast the spell and have the following Magickal ingredients ready and placed on your altar.

You'll see from the ingredients list this spell invites you to work with Crystal Magick for the first time, but don't worry if you don't have a small citrine. If you do, use it because it is the crystal that manifests abundance—both more money and greater personal power:

Magickal Ingredients

Small spell jar with a lid/cork

Pine incense for consecration/purifying the jar

A fresh pomegranate, cut in half and a small pin to pick out individual seeds

An oak branch with oak leaves or, if this is not feasible, a drawing of an oak branch with leaves

Gold altar candle to signify abundance and wealth heading your way

Dried Lavender

Dried Mint

Fresh mint and a strainer or, if this is not possible, a herbal mint tea bag

Your chalice and a kettle to make mint tea

1 small cinnamon stick

1 small citrine (yellow) crystal

Pinch of dried marigold flowers (you can find these in good health stores)

A posy of fresh marigold flowers to decorate your altar (again, if you can't find these then just do a simple drawing to depict this symbol of improved fortunes.)

To cast your spell

There are several steps to this spell; try to enjoy each one and don't be tempted to rush through to the end. Once you have cast your circle, take all the time you need.

Light your incense and cleanse/consecrate the spell jar you have chosen for this spell in its smoke.

Now cast your circle, and remember to thank your Divine Helpers for accepting your invitation and joining you.

Step (1) Make the mint tea in your chalice

Mint helps us manifest more money, more luck, and more chances to travel. Allow your brew to cool enough to drink it, and as you wait for that, state your intent out loud. Say these words:

> *"If it pleases, I am now open to Abundance and ready to receive my share of more [**state here what it is you would like more of**], and since I am now ready, please send it to me."*

You may be asking for abundance in just one area of your life, but this spell gives you the opportunity to ask four times and if you wish, you can ask for abundance in four different areas of your life. You might ask for more money, the chance to travel more, an opportunity to meet more people, or just more happiness. There is no right or wrong. Ask for what you know you need more of and try to be specific.

Step (2) Pick out (with the pin) the pomegranate seeds and eat them

The pomegranate and its seeds bring us blessings and more clarity, so if you are unsure what other areas of your life you would like to invite abundance into, think about your choices as you mindfully eat some of the pomegranate seeds as part of this spell. When you are ready, say out loud:

> *"If it pleases, I am now open to Abundance and ready to receive my share of more [**state here what it is you would like more of**], and since I am now ready, please send it to me."*

Step (3) Fill the Spell Jar

All of the Magickal ingredients you have prepared on your altar will work together to encourage abundance into your life but how you fill the Spell Jar with them is entirely up to you. You can mix them all up and pour the mix into the jar or you can do what I like to do which is to build layers of the different dried herbs and flowers. When the jar is half full, tuck the small citrine crystal into the dried herbs and carry on filling the jar and covering the crystal. If the jar is too small for the cinnamon, then just snap the stick and use a flake.

Before you go to the final step of sealing the spell, place the open jar on your altar. Point your wand at the jar and say the following words out loud:

*"If it pleases, I am now open to Abundance and ready to receive my share of more [**state here what it is you would like more of**], and since I am now ready, please send it to me."*

Step (4) Seal the jar

Seal the spell jar by replacing the lid or cork and now carefully tilt your Golden candle to cover the lid/cork in a wax coating. A gold candle represents wealth and leadership; and so, this too is a ritual way of sealing Magick into the jar. As you seal your Spell Jar, say out loud one final time:

*"If it pleases, I am now open to Abundance and ready to receive my share of more [**state here***

***what it is you would like more of]**, and since I am now ready, please send it to me."*

Once the wax has cooled and set, your Abundance Spell Jar is finished, and your spell is complete.

Thank your Divine Helpers and close the circle.

Keep the jar close by but out of view and hidden. Don't talk about it. Don't keep picking it up to inspect it. Leave the Magick to work in its own time, and remember, patience is a virtue—and this spell is already bringing you more of that as you wait for greater abundance to unfold in your life.

Chapter Six: Spells for Friendship

If you want to cast a spell for friendship it might be worth thinking about what it is that you are really asking for before you start. Have you moved to a new area or changed work and relocated which means you don't know anyone locally? Or, have the friendships you have enjoyed until now hit their 'expiry' date? Do you feel you have less and less in common with those you may have shared some of your childhood with or your school days?

Why do you want new/more friends? Are you seeking someone who can share your new Wicca path or at least understand why Magick and an Earth-centered faith is important to you?

When we start to work with Magick it is helpful to us—and the Divine Helpers who want us to be happy and get what we want and need—to know specifically what we are asking for. Once you have the answer, then you'll enjoy casting this friendship spell and waiting for it to take root in your life.

If you think about it, you've probably been working with friendship Magick since childhood. Did you ever swap friendship bracelets with someone? If that's not symbolic of 'the ties that bind' and in this case 'bind in friendship' then I don't know what is. Even the birthday gifts you may have exchanged with friends were symbolic of a connection that, at the time, was meaningful for both parties with bonds that were beyond words.

Friendship spells are a joy, and your Divine Helpers will be clamoring to join you once your circle has been cast. Don't be surprised if one or two new ones show up—the Magick itself may be serious, but that doesn't mean your helpers don't know how to have fun! Especially the faery folk that may have been hovering on the edge of your Magickal tribe until now, just waiting for their opportunity to step up and step in to help you out.

A friend is someone who is a stranger until you both meet and say hello. And with that in mind, this spell weaves together your energy with those you may not yet have met. You may be doing the Magickal weaving (literally in this spell), but it will be your Divine Helpers who will know when the time is right for these energies to meet and make friends. So, as ever, you do your bit—and allow them to do theirs!

A Spell for Friendship

The best day to spells that bind good and loving friendships is Saturday

Ingredients

Bracelet threads in the following colors: you can use thread, ribbons, wool or thin strips of fabric. The choice is yours, what matters more are the colors, as listed here:

Red – For Life

Orange – For Healing Friendships

Yellow – For Happy friendships

Green – For Nature

Blue – For Harmony in Friendships

Purple – For Spiritual Friendships

Cut each thread or fabric strip to a length that will comfortably wrap three times around your wrist, once plaited. It is better to overestimate the length because you can always trim the plait itself.

You will also need a purple altar candle for this spell. Purple signifies the things we know even when we don't know how or why. This often plays out in friendships—you may meet someone, connect instantly and then discover you share a similar experience of childhood. You didn't consciously know this when you met but on a psychic level, you recognized each other. We call this 'resonance', and it is an instinct you can develop as you become a more skilled witch.

Lavender oil for the incense burner

Cloves and honey to make clove tea in your chalice and sweeten it to your taste

A spring of willow (or a photo/drawing you if you have no access to the living plant)

Peaceful music to accompany your weaving

To cast your Friendship spell

As always, prepare everything you will need for your Friendships spells before you cast your circle—And, as ever, invite your Divine Helpers to join you for this spell.

Light the incense burner and allow the scent of lavender to pervade the room; lavender signifies love and what you will be asking for is loving friendships. You want to attract people who lift you up, not people who pull you down so that they feel better about themselves!

Make the clove tea, strain, and pour into your scared chalice. Cloves represent protection from negative people, including friends who have started behaving in unkind ways towards you! You can also sweeten/temper this tea with honey to more positively represent how good friendship makes our lives sweeter. Take a sip of the tea and then say the following words aloud:

"If it pleases, I am now open to new Loving Friendships and ready to give and receive my share of the happiness and support that good friendships bring. Since I am now ready, please send it to me."

You are now going to sit quietly in your Magickal Circle and weave your threads/ribbons into a 'Friendship' bracelet that you are gifting to yourself to remind you that you have cast a powerful spell to attract new friends into your life; and so, you will need to stay open to that possibility when you meet new people.

Once you have plaited (woven) the bracelet, place it on the altar underneath the sprig of willow (or the image of that plant). Willow represents the ties that bind.

Point your wand at the bracelet—which is really now a Magickal Talisman—and repeat the same intent as before.

Wrap this Magickal talisman around your left wrist three times to remind you, always, of the Wicca Rule of Three and say the words.

"So, mote it be"

The spell is now complete.

Thank all your divine helpers, close the circle and don't take your bracelet off, except to bathe or shower or swim. It will, when the time is right, bring that which you have asked for in the shape of Loving New Friends.

Protection from Unkind Friends

The best day for spells that are self-empowering is Sunday

We saw in the above spell how clove will protect you from unkind friends. You can also use the candle magic you learned in earlier chapters to move an unkind friend away from you. Use a black candle which represents protection and clearing negativity.

Stud the tops of the candle with cloves and then carve the name of the person who has wounded you into the wax. Remember to write from the top down to move their energy away from you.

Unless it is urgent that you act straight away, try to wait for the waning moon to do this spell. Any time after the Full Moon and before the New Moon will work.

As you cast this spell and move this person's negative energy away from yours, do so with loving kindness. You are not trying to harm this person, or any other (remember the Rule of Three?), you just need their toxic energy moved away from you so you can focus on the things that do bring happiness and light into your life.

When your spell is done, close your circle, thank your divine helpers and go and bury the candle stub somewhere private but outside of your home.

Chapter Seven: Spells for Peace & The Planet

Most of the spells we've done so far have been spells in which you state your personal intent or desire and place those wishes into the invisible 'hands' of your Divine Helpers, including the Goddess.

In this chapter, we are going to cast our Magickal net a little wider and explore spell casting for the good of the collective—not only our communities but Mother Earth and the planet we live on.

You would have to have had your head stuck in a bucket of sand—Ostrich-style—not to know, after 50 years of relentless mining and polluting and big business agriculture, that the planet is not in the greatest shape. So, anything we can do, individually and collectively to try and undo some of the harm that's been done will always be welcomed by the planet and her invisible helpers and guardians.

So, this is the chapter where we turn our Wiccan gaze outwards and ask: How can I help? What Magick can I call on to heal past wrongs, not only between peoples but between the planet and her two-legged inhabitants?

Let's start with some spells to send peace where it is needed most. As we cast this spell, we simply create the Magickal energy that helps promote peace—we may not know where it is needed most, we will leave that decision to the wisdom of our Divine Helpers who will know where to send it.

Before we start the spell, go online and find an image of Picasso's Peace Dove. There are numerous representations of the dove as a symbol of peace; but you might like to focus on Picasso's drawing because this was the one that was adopted by the Peace Movement in 1949 and used as the symbol for the first-ever international peace conference.

Once you've found it, download and print it to use in your sacred space or, if the muse grabs you, get creative and draw your own version ready to use in your peace-promoting spells.

Feather Magick

This is not a spell to rush and not least because you need something else that you might have to wait to come to you: You need two bird feathers.

These don't have to come from fancy birds—there's no need to go online and spend a week's wages on a shamanic eagle feather or one from a wise old owl (although you could add either of those to your birthday wish-list when the time comes). Just keep your eyes peeled and these special feathers will find you.

I know of one Hedgerow witch who never told a soul that she followed the Wiccan path (this was some twenty years ago and people where she lived were a bit less tolerant of pagan ways back then). Anyway, she went out one morning to do something distinctly non-Wiccan—like go to the family food shop—and when she returned home there was the most enormous bird of prey feather lying on the carpet in her hallway.

Nope, there were no windows left open; Nobody had been in or out of the house in her absence and there was no way—other than a Magickal way—this feather could have found its way into her home.

I'm not saying the same will happen to you—we all share the Wiccan path, but our footsteps are not the same. I am saying you can trust that because you need feathers for this next spell, feathers will find you. Don't worry if they don't match; or come from the same bird; or are different colors. None of this matters when you are starting out.

That said, here is a quick at-a-glance chart of Feather Magick colors and what they mean. If you like this type of Magick and find yourself drawn to it more than, say, candle Magick you might want to start to collect feathers and even do a spell asking your Divine Helpers to help the right feathers find you.

My friend who found the feather in her hallway immediately switched from a willow wand to using the feather in the same way. She had long studied shamanic traditions and so it made sense the feather would become her main sacred tool!

Feather Colors Symbology

White: Purification, spirituality, hope, protection and peace; moon blessings

Green: Money, fertility, growth

Brown: Health, stability, grounding your home space

Orange: Attraction, energy, success

Yellow: Intelligence, blessings of the sun

Red: Courage, good fortune, life

Pink: Love

Grey: Peace

Blue: Psychic awareness, peace and health

Black: Don't use these if you are a beginner!

Red & Brown: healing animals

Brown & White: Happiness

Gray & White: Hope and balance

Wiccans all over the world join together every year at Lammas—August 1—to cast a collective spell for peace. You can easily join in just by casting your circle and lighting a white candle too.

A beginner's spell for peace

Ingredients

Feathers x2

Golden thread

Golden candle

Picture of drawing of Picasso's Peace Dove symbol

Dried bay leaves

Lavender oil

Thyme

Streaming device to play John Rutter's composition, A *Gaelic Blessing** after your incantation (you can download this music or find it on YouTube).

*This is a hymn in the Christian tradition and so the lyrics talk about Christ, but you can imagine this as an alternate Divine Energy that speaks to you.

To cast your spell for peace

Clean, tidy and prepare your Magickal working space. Now, your altar is ready to cast this spell.

Make sure you can see your Peace Dove symbol and that you have everything else you need at hand, so you won't have to break the circle once cast.

Invite your Divine Helpers to join you and tell them this is a shared intent—for the greater good, not just your own. That will determine who shows up to help you.

Cast your circle and light the lavender oil. Allow yourself a few moments to really absorb and enjoy its heady scent—lavender symbolizes peace and protection and love!

Now you are ready for the Feather Magick.

Sit quietly in your Magickal Circle and join the two feathers that have found you by tying their quill ends with the golden thread. Gold is the color of leadership which is why you are also using a golden candle.

Without great global leadership, nothing will change so this color is important in this spell.

Once you have tied your feathers together light the gold candle and tilt it to spill a little wax over the golden thread and reinforce this binding.

Now you are ready to state your intent.

Say out loud:

"I know that it pleases and so I am asking all here to help deliver peace where it is most needed. I offer these feathers as a symbol of that peace but also the swiftness with which we can change so that nobody needs to live in fear and we can stop destroying one another.

Great Goddess, please know I am ready to know work in whatever way I can—both in and out of this Magickal Circle—to help you and all your helpers to bring peace to all."

Now say:

"So, mote it be"

After this incantation you can play the beautiful Gaelic blessing. Hold the bound feathers in both hands, keep your focus on them as a symbol of peace and really listen to the words.

The final part of the spell is to write your message of peace on one of the dried bay leaves—bay, you will recall, is used in manifestation spells. Write your message and then (carefully) burn your leaf in the flame of the golden (leadership) candle.

Your Peace Spell is now cast, and you can thank your helpers, including the birds who donated the feathers you have used. Blow out your candle and keep your feathers on the altar to encourage peace to run through all your Magickal Works.

A healing spell for the planet

In most rituals, Wiccans will honor both The God and the Goddess, which is why I have linked these spells for peace and for the planet. In asking for peace, you have involved the Goddess and her helpers. As we now ask for healing for the planet, we will turn to her consort, The God, who, as we learned in chapter one, is strongly associated with nature and wilderness.

His symbol is The Sun or The Stag (hence his commonly-used name, The Horned One); so decide which of these symbols speaks to you and make sure to involve it in this ritual.

We are going outdoors for this spell. Don't worry if you live in the middle of a busy city, once you start looking, you'll find signs of nature everywhere and one of these will call to you. You will know you've been 'called' because you have noticed this tree or shrub or lonely daisy pushing up through a pavement crack.

Since we are heading outdoors for part of this healing spell, we are going to first consecrate the tools and Magickal Talismans we will be using indoors at our altar before we step outside. If you can head to the countryside or out into the wilderness then do so; go to a favorite spot. If you can head where there is running water it is even better because water, like Magick itself, is in constant motion.

This is a multi-step spell so make sure you have everything you need before you start. You will do some of the spell indoors and some outdoors. Since we need, collectively, more care and concern for our planet and those who share it, try and complete all these activities as the moon is waxing, so between the New and the Full Moons.

Indoors

Plant a seed

You can plant anything but you're going to keep this plant on your altar as a sign of the life force and the energy of the Horned God so don't plant a giant redwood tree! You are going to consecrate this plant, along with the other items you will be using in this multi-step spell, and then—as a symbol of what the planet now needs—you are going to give it all the love and care it requires to thrive. It needs water, it needs warmth and, once germinated, it needs sunlight to make the nutrients it needs to grow strong and healthy. Take away any one of those three and your seed will do its very best to grow but it will fail—the stem may be too long and spindly, the leaves may yellow. As you tend to your new plants, be mindful this is the kind of dedicated care our planet now needs.

Dry a leaf

Bring a leaf from outside indoors—any leaf that finds its way to you. After you have consecrated this leaf, you are going to dry it. One of the best ways to do this is to place it between layers of old newspaper and put it under the carpet. Over time, the leaf will dry, and you will have a symbol of senescence—of the natural end of the life cycle; the ebb and flow of life and the natural rhythms that our human activity too often disrupts. This then is your symbol of transformation when a cycle is allowed to complete itself. Nature is not afraid of death and we need not be either. But, the destruction of our planet for greed is not the same thing!

Outdoors

Next time you are outdoors, keep an eye out for a stone. Any stone. A stone that 'speaks' to you. Bring your stone indoors and put it with the plant and the leaf so you can consecrate all three together when you have cast your Magickal circle. The plant and the leaf will stay on the altar, but the stone will be returned to nature. The stone represents an immutable force. Unlike the rest of us, it is not going anywhere. This is your symbol of the power of the Horned God and the life force of the planet itself.

Your final preparation is to buy a beautiful bunch of flowers. Keep them alive in a vase until we are ready to start the spell, after this it will be only the flower heads that you need.

Casting your spell

Step (1) – Indoors-Consecration

Consecrate your plant; your leaf (dry the leaf after the ritual), your stone and your flowers. Call in your Divine Helpers and ask in particular that The Horned God come and work with you.

Cast your circle and honor his power and presence by lighting a Green candle, representing nature, and placing his symbol—the sun or the stag, or whatever you have chosen, alongside.

Now, state your intent as follows. Say, out loud:

"Great Lord, as the sun and the moon shine on this land bless us with a vision of how to live in harmony with each other and with the earth we all share.

Bless this land and give us your vision of how to do this.

Send us the wisdom of the ancestors and of the wilderness.

May all be blessed.

May all receive, according to fairness and their needs.

When you are ready, thank your Divine Helpers and close the circle.

When you can next go outside, go and bury your consecrated stone. It has been blessed by Magick and carries your intent back into the earth. The planet will know this.

Find a way to send your consecrated flower heads down a river/stream, or out to sea, or to the middle of a lake. Like the stone, they carry your healing intent back to source.

As you bury your stone and scatter your flowers, say quietly to yourself:

"So, mote it be"

Chapter Eight: Celebrating the Sabbats

Sabbats are the sacred days or festivals that witches celebrate, and on the eve of each of these days, you can prepare yourself and your Magickal workspace for the 'Big Day' ahead by cleaning and tidying your altar; and decorating it in a way that is symbolic of the festival you are about to celebrate.

Wiccans celebrate eight sabbats in total, which mark either the start or the midpoint of each of the four seasons: Spring, Summer, Autumn, and Winter. Remember, Wicca has deep roots in the English and European traditions of the 'Craft of the Wise' and so the natural cycles celebrated are those of the Northern Hemisphere.

The names of the sabbats are:

- Imbolg
- Eostre/Spring Equinox
- Beltane
- Litha/Summer Solstice
- Lughnasadh/Lammas
- Mabon/Autumn Equinox
- Samhain/Halloween
- Yule/Winter Solstice

Some of these days—Christmas and Easter, and the Summer and Winter solstices, for instance—are marked and celebrated by people of no particular religion or faith because, thanks to their strong pagan roots, they have survived across the centuries and been absorbed into the secular Christian calendar.

For Wiccans, these are important dates because they mark all the natural cycles that we reconnect with once we start practicing modern Wiccan Magick.

Here are the dates of each of these important festivals, together with their symbolism. With this information you can choose how you would like to celebrate each festival and honor those natural cycles that make up the ebb and flow of all life and connect you to the Web of Life.

Imbolg - February 2

Purification & Inspiration

The land is being prepared for spring to burst forth. Even if you live in the city, you can watch this happening by taking a walk in the park and looking at the buds on the trees lining your street.

Eostre - also called Spring Equinox, March 21

Fertility & Re-emergence

We begin to emerge from the darkness of a long winter and celebrate a renewed self. We've moved out of the dark and into the light. This is a time to cast spells of gratitude and great hope for the unfurling year.

Beltane - May 1

Love & Union

This is the Festival of Love, and it may be that you grew up in a tradition where you or your ancestors danced around the Maypole with the pole representing the male and the ribbons representing the female. You were probably never told this, but this ritual was a symbol of making love in the great outdoors! This is a great time to cast any of those true love spells from chapter three.

Litha/Summer Solstice

Happiness & Fulfilment

Life is good. There is more light in the Northern Hemisphere than at any other time of the year and this alone is worth a celebration before we start the long march back to shorter days and winter cycles. If ever there was a time to party, this is it. Cast your spells for friendship and good luck.

Lughnasadh/Lammas - August 1

Transformation & Early Harvest

There's a tinge of sadness as we start to notice the days getting shorter, but nature compensates by giving us a taste of the harvest to come. There is work ahead—the coming crops will need harvesting and preparing for storage, but this is also a time we can think about sharing the bounty that comes our way. This is a great time to cast the spells for abundance and healing for the planet.

Mabon/Autumn Equinox - September 21 to 29

Thanksgiving & Harvest

This can also be a time of reflection of the year that has unfurled as we gather our harvest—and this does not just mean food resources, it can mean money and spiritual growth too—safely in for the dark days and nights of winter that loom ahead. A time for spells of thanksgiving.

Samhain/Halloween - October 31

Death & Rebirth

A time to think about who and what has gone before. Halloween has been hijacked by commercialism but has deep roots in the Pagan beliefs of our ancestors. They say that on All Hallows Eve as it is also known, the veil between this world and the next becomes so thin you can make the connections with your ancestors that you might wish to. This is a time to cast spells asking for guidance from those who have gone before you.

Yule/Winter Solstice - December 21

Birth & New Hope

With the Christian tradition of Christmas just a few days later, this really is the season where birth and new hope is celebrated by many. Even those with no secular faith or spiritual traditions pass in the street wishing each other peace and prosperity and goodwill and joy. The Goddess promises a new start and we gratefully accept that gift. This is the time to cast your peace spells to great effect.

Conclusion

If you have worked your way through all the previous chapters in this book and practiced these beginner's spells, then you will now have the know-how, and hopefully the growing confidence, to begin making Wicca and its traditions a part of your everyday life!

Just remember: *So, mote it be...*

www.ingramcontent.com/pod-product-compliance
Lightning Source LLC
LaVergne TN
LVHW011740060526
838200LV00051B/3267